W9-BZX-465

HOW COINS AND BILLS ARE MADE

MONEY POWER

Jason Cooper

Rourke
Publishing LLC
Vero Beach, Florida 32964

www.rourkepublishing.com

PHOTO CREDITS: © Department of the Treasury Bureau of Engraving and Printing; © East Coast Studios; ©The Federal Reserve System; © Official U.S. Mint Photograph; © James P. Rowan; © The Smithsonian Institution National Numismatic Collection; © Lynn M. Stone

Editor: Frank Sloan

Cover Photo: *Checking there are no mistakes before a new bill is printed.*

Cover design by Nicola Stratford

Library of Congress Cataloging-in-Publication Data

Cooper, Jason
   How coins and bills are made / Jason Cooper
     p. cm. — (Money power)
   Includes bibliographical references and index.
   Summary: Describes the steps involved in minting coins and paper money, and touches on the topics of coin collecting and deterring counterfeiters.
   ISBN 1-58952-211-7
   1. Money—Juvenile literature. [1. Money.] I. Title.

HG221.5 .C664 2002
686.2'88—dc21
                                   2001048910

Printed in the USA

G/CG

TABLE OF CONTENTS

ALBERT GALLATIN

WHO MAKES MONEY?

The dollars and cents that make up United States **currency**, or cash money, are **manufactured** in buildings. Those buildings are run by the United States Department of the Treasury in Washington, D.C.

The Treasury Department is made up of many parts. One is called the U.S. **Mint**. Another is known as the Bureau of Engraving and Printing.

A statue of Albert Gallatin in front of the U. S. treasury building. Gallatin was appointed secretary of the Treasury in 1801.

COINS AND BILLS

The job of the mint is to make, or mint, coins and medals. The main mint is in Washington, D.C. Coins are also made at mints in Philadelphia, Denver, and San Francisco.

The Bureau of Engraving and Printing's job is to make paper money. Paper money is also known as bills, or Federal Reserve Notes. The Bureau is in Washington, D.C.

U. S. coins: pennies, nickels, dimes, and quarters

DESIGNING COINS

Before coins can be minted, they must be designed. The person who approves the design of a coin is the secretary of the treasury. This is the person who is in charge of the Treasury Department.

Old coins and a bill. Designs and models were made before the money was made.

COIN MODELS

A coin must be made in model form before it can be minted. The first model is made from soft wax. A second model is made from plaster of Paris. In the second model, details can be added to the design. A third, final model is made from **epoxy**. Epoxy begins as a wet substance, but it dries into a very hard substance.

The final design is cut into metal **dies**. One die has the imprint of the front of the coin. The other die has the back.

An epoxy model of the official President Clinton medal

MINTING COINS

The mint makes its coins from strips of metal. Machines called blanking presses punch out coin shapes from the strips of metal. You can think of the blanking press as a cookie cutter that cuts metal!

Before they are stamped with words and designs, coins are called **blanks**. Blanks are given grooved edges through a process called **milling**. They are also heated so that they are soft for stamping.

Rolls of thin metal strips are used to make coin blanks.

The dies strike the coin blanks. One die stamps the front of the coin. At the same time, the other die stamps the back.

Some blanks are struck with 170 tons (154.5 metric tons) of pressure. That force is equal to the weight of 21 adult elephants!

Blank coins are struck with metal dies that produce the coin.

SPECIAL COINS

The U.S. Mint makes some of its coins for collectors. The collection or study of coins is called **numismatics**.

Coins made for collectors are polished. They are known as proof coins. Collectors like the shiny proof coins because they have never been handled.

Many old coins are very valuable. Some of the first American coins were silver half-cents. Some of them are now worth more than $20,000!

The U. S. Mint stopped making the Susan B. Anthony dollar coin because people confused it with a quarter!

Many bills were given new designs in the 1990s.

Many machines are used in the printing of paper money.

MAKING PAPER MONEY

Engravers cut the design of a bill onto a die. The design of a paper bill is then transferred to a printing plate. The printing plate is part of a printing press.

Printing presses at the Bureau of Engraving and Printing print paper money on sheets of special paper. There are 32 bills on each sheet of paper.

The process takes several days. The green ink on the back of bills must dry before the front can be printed.

This printing press holds the plate that prints the back side of a dollar bill.

NEW BILLS

The design of American paper money sometimes changes. In 1996, for example, the $100 bill was given a new design. The picture of Benjamin Franklin was made larger. It was also moved to the left. To the right of Franklin, a **watermark** was added. A watermark is a small design in the paper. It can be seen only when held up to light.

Since 1996 most of the other bills have been changed as well. New bills are designed in ways to make them harder for **counterfeiters** to copy.

GLOSSARY

blank (BLANK) — a metal coin before it has been stamped

counterfeiter (KOWN tur FIT uhr) — a person who makes fake money

currency (KER en see) — cash money

die (DYE) — an object used to stamp or shape another object

engraver (en GRAYV uhr) — one who cuts figures or designs into a die or plate, often for printing

epoxy (eh POK see) — a substance that changes from liquid to solid as it dries

manufacture (man yoo FAK chur) — to use machinery to make or produce something

milling (MIL ing) — the process in which grooves are cut into a metal surface

mint (MINT) — a building where coins are made; to make, or manufacture, coins

numismatics (NOO mez MAT iks) — the study or collection of rare and unusual coins and bills

watermark (WAH tur mark) — a hard-to-see mark or design stamped into paper

INDEX

Further Reading

Abeyta, Jennifer. *Coins*. Children's Press, 2000

Websites To Visit

http://www.frbsf.org/currency/index.html
http://www.moneyfactory.com

About The Author

Jason Cooper has written several children's books about a variety of topics for Rourke Publishing, including recent series *China Discovery* and *American Landmarks*. Cooper travels widely to gather information for his books. Two of his favorite travel destinations are Alaska and the Far East.